Do as I Say, Not as I Did

Do as I Say, Not as I Did

*A Self-Deprecating Reflection on Life to Help
Others Succeed*

Diane DiPiero Rodio

Parafine Press

First Parafine Press Edition 2020
ISBN: 978-1-950843-34-3

Parafine Press
www.parafinepress.com

Book design by David Wilson
Cover design by David Wilson

Table of Contents

"FORWARD"

That spelling was intentional.

Don't think of this as the beginning of a book—a *foreword*. This is the beginning of your life away from your home base. You are moving *forward*. You are growing up. And in that march toward independence, you will likely look to those who have gone before you for sage advice and examples of enlightened living.

You won't get that here.

Instead, I have taken it upon myself to recall the more humiliating, face-palm moments of my life as vivid illustrations of how not to go about achieving success and/or inner joy. This act of selflessness on my part should not be taken lightly. Each nonsensical act should be met with a laugh but also with a distinct understanding that you must do exactly the opposite of what I did. With the benefit of hindsight, I can more clearly see these missteps, and, for the sake of posterity, fully realize how things really should have been done. I can't relive my life, so the onus is on you.

Do as I say, not as I did.

P.S.—Please don't feel sorry for me. The fact that I can remember my mistakes means there weren't all that many of them. There's been more good than bad, more right than wrong. This book wouldn't be half as interesting, though, if I wrote about everything I did correctly. So sit back and enjoy, but be sure to pay attention!

CHAPTER 1
DON'T YOU EVER DOUBT YOURSELF

Have you ever seen people who make mistakes and don't care? They'll say something completely wrong in class or drive in the opposite direction of where they should be going, and they just shrug their shoulders and say, "Oh well." They believe in themselves enough to realize it's okay to make a few mistakes.

Now here's the difference between those people and me. "*Oh hell*" is what I would have said.

"*Oh hell,* am I stupid."

"*Oh hell,* everyone thinks I'm an idiot."

"*Oh hell,* I'm never going to speak in class/drive again."

What kind of an attitude is that? A really bad one. An attitude that eats away at your self-confidence and gives others the impression that you're too wrapped up in yourself.

I used to think that I worried too much about what other people thought, but really I was worrying too much about what *I thought* other people were thinking about me. I hope you follow what I'm saying. Don't become so consumed with your perceptions of yourself or of how you envision others seeing you that you silence your thoughts and deprive others of the amazing talents you have. Don't deprive them of the chance to see you make a mistake *and laugh about it.*

I wish someone had given me this advice when I was younger.

During my years with a magazine in New York, we had monthly idea meetings. Everyone was encouraged to come prepared with at least two story ideas related to design and architecture. Some people (the overachievers) showed up in the editor's office with a thick file of information related to the half-dozen ideas they breathlessly shared. Others (the kiss-ups) came empty-handed but were able to pull an idea out of thin air and sell it to the editor.

Then you had me. I might have had an idea or two every once in a while, but was I going to share them in front of everyone and risk the humiliation of being told that they were half-baked? Of course not. I just smiled and nodded at people's ideas and looked down at my nails anytime the editor started to scan the room, in case he thought about calling on me. I know, how very "ninth grade" of me.

My line of thinking at the time was, "I don't want to appear dumb to these people." So, how did I appear to them after not taking part in a brainstorming session? Yeah, probably dumb. They all knew I wasn't, of course, because I was a good and reliable writer, but I certainly didn't come across as the type of confident person who could actually drum up the ideas for articles she'd like to write.

Ugh. When I look back on that, I want to jump into the past and throttle myself. "What are you doing? You look like an idiot, just the thing you didn't want! Say something, anything. Suggest a story on turnpike restroom design, for Pete's sake. At least you'd get a laugh out of people."

YOU are not going to go down this path. Not if I can help it. The strength within you has to propel you forward and drown out the negative voices in your head. Speak up. Say something, as long as it's pertinent to the topic. Sometimes you will feel this little burning inside of you, and it's not indigestion. It's the realization that a great thought has come to you and it should be shared.

Share it. If it falls on deaf ears, it either needs to be refined or the people with whom you shared it don't recognize your brilliance. Don't squash that great idea. Share it with someone else. Hold on to it for the future. Do not tell yourself that your concept was dumb—or that you are dumb. You just haven't found the right audience. Or maybe this is just the germ of a fantastic idea that will come into full bloom with time. You will never know unless you speak up. And in order to speak up, you have to believe in yourself.

Self-confidence will take you far in life. It's the gift that will tell you when to take action in the classroom, in the workplace, and in the world. Understand that being confident is not being full of yourself, which is something I used to think. "Who does that woman think she is, sharing her opinion with higher-ups and getting involved in all sorts of projects around the office?" She *knows* she is someone with an inquisitive mind, with creative ideas, and with the desire to grow. That's not being full of yourself; that's believing in yourself.

Self-confidence can come in dribs and drabs or like a ball shooting out of a cannon. Try to get somewhere in-between to find your comfort zone. Personally, I had the self-confidence to attend an out-of-state university; I had the self-confidence to study abroad for a semester; and I had the self-confidence to pack my bags three weeks after graduating from college and move to New York City. I felt very brave, and I was.

But then my self-confidence kind of fizzled. I was working as an assistant editor at a national magazine. How should I use self-confidence to learn and grow? (More on that later.) I was in Italy for four months. How could I immerse myself in the language and culture, besides eating pizza and drinking wine?

You can lose your self-confidence at the most crucial times. Once you've achieved a small portion of your goal, you can't back down. I learned that, finally, when I left New York for Cleveland. I was so proud of myself for driving across three states in a 15-foot rental truck with a Subaru hitched to the back. (More on that, too.) My old self would have caved there and not pushed herself farther. But I got a part-time proofreading job and threw my name around as a freelance writer. It took a lot of work, and some rejection, to reach my goals. And let me tell you, it felt really good when I did.

Very often, confidence won't drastically change your life, but it will always make you feel good about yourself. It can also help others feel good at the same time. I find myself remembering a particular ride on a New Jersey Transit train from my apartment to my job in Manhattan. I was reading a book by an Irish writer. It was a very clever little tome, even though I did not understand all of the Irish nuances. I was engrossed in my book when the train halted at the next stop and a man sat across from me. I was doing a good job of not paying attention to him, for fear he'd engage me in conversation. But then he said, in an adorable Irish accent, "Do you like that book?"

I looked up for a moment. I smiled. I said, "Yes, I do." And then I went back to reading my book.

This seemingly nice Irish gentleman no doubt thought I was a cold American, not interested in striking up a conversation with a handsome Irish stranger. On the contrary, I was fumbling through my portfolio of conversation starters, each one sounding dumber to me than the other.

Have you read this book? It's really good. No, that sounds too simplistic.

What's the last book you read? Oh lord, you sound like a nerd.

Thank goodness you're here! Can you help me translate some of the Irish stuff? Way too forward to say to someone you don't know.

No, don't say that; that's stupid. You can't say something like that; he'll think you're flirting with him. Why would you want to say *that?*

So I said nothing at all.

Nothing!

Inside, my head was screaming out sentences to keep the dialogue going, but my lack of self-confidence had me convinced that anything I thought of saying was ridiculous. It has been years and years since this event, yet I can still picture him exiting the train in Hoboken. At that moment, everything I wanted to say was on the tip of my tongue, and of course it was too late.

Every time I think about this seemingly innocuous event, I squirm. And I think about it a lot more than you might imagine. Why? Early on, I illogically worried that the man on the train might have been my future husband, but I let him go. After that, I started to worry that I was actually a mean person, someone who didn't care to show a little kindness to others. Finally, I moved on to kicking myself for not letting words leave my mouth over fear that I'd say something stupid.

To this day, it makes me so uncomfortable to think that I lacked the basic confidence to just talk to someone. Part of it was shyness, I know. But once someone talks to you, it seems only natural you'd talk back. That is, of course, if you believe in yourself enough to do so. That would not be the last time I let myself down, but it remains one of the most vivid reminders of how lack of confidence frustrated me.

To make up for such past occurrences, I now speak to just about anyone. I will strike up a conversation with the plumber, the cashier at Target, the receptionist at the dentist's office. This has occasionally made my children's eyes roll, but I really don't care. I feel much better speaking to people than wondering if I'm smart enough to carry on a conversation.

When you start to feel like you're losing self-confidence, find someone who believes in you and listen to them. I wish I had that done years ago. In fact, I am very good at making other people feel great about themselves, and lousy about doing the same for myself. I could hear people telling me that I was smart, that I had great things to say, and that I should be more confident, but I was still drowning in a sea of personal negativity. So I'm going to tell you this right now: When someone tells you that you're awesome, you believe them! It's not arrogant to think that they're right; it's allowing yourself to see what others see in you, and to let that positivity shine through.

On the flip side, there will be days when you can't find a soul who seems to believe in you. They're either not understanding what you're saying or they're caught up in their own thoughts, and it will feel like you're going it alone. And so you must. If your mind and your heart and your conscience tell you that what you are doing is right, then that's all the motivation required. Believe in yourself, even when it feels like no one else does. Even when you're not sure it's worth it. Because it is.

CHAPTER 2
REMEMBER, IT'S NOT ABOUT YOU

Well, that's a bummer.

I mean, it's your life, isn't it? So, why shouldn't the world revolve around you and your happiness?

The fact is, your happiness is locked up in everyone else's. Your ability to help others will in turn make you think less about yourself while at the same time lead you toward fulfillment.

It's a delicate balance. If you set out to please all the people all the time, you're likely to burn out, become resentful, or forget the difference between being good and being a pushover. Then, when you realize you were letting people take too much from you, you try to turn it around and you end up looking like a selfish jerk. Oh yeah, I've been there.

"You're too easy," my father would say to me. (Not easy like *that*. Easy in the sense that I was too nice to people and thus let some take advantage of me.) He was not mistaken. I had this notion that if I was overly nice to people, they would like me and the love would flow right back to me.

Here is a mild example:

When I was really young, I had long, thick, wavy red hair. Some of the girls at school liked to play hairdresser, using me as their client. They would lift up the tresses in the back and "tease" my hair with a comb. I thought this was great fun. The other reason I did this was that I really wanted people to like me, and I assumed that letting them play with my hair would make these girls my friends.

What it actually made was a mess. With vivid detail, I can recall my mother attempting to undo the thick knots of hair that developed along the nape. These clumps were too much for Johnson & Johnson's "No More Tangles." My mother had to cut them out of my head.

"Don't let them tease your hair like that," she would say, and a few days later, I'd let them tease my hair like that again. It should come as no surprise that I was not gaining much traction in the friendship department. These girls were simply having a blast destroying my auburn locks.

And one evening, it was all too much for my mother. After playing tug-of-war with the knots, a losing battle for her that left both of us in tears, my mother made the dreadful announcement: "You're getting a haircut."

This had to be around 1974, the height of long hair. No one got hair*cuts*. You just kept growing it until it reached your bum, and then maybe you trimmed it ever so slightly to avoid split ends. But the hippy look was coming to a close for this youngster. My mother dragged me to the J.C. Penney hair salon at the Southern Park Mall in Boardman, Ohio, and told the stylist to take off several inches.

I cried through the whole experience, and when it was done I had a *shag*. My lovely long locks were shredded into tiny layers. I barely looked like myself. The stylist, sensing that she had quite possibly ruined my life, delicately handed me 6 inches of hair. I wrapped the tresses in paper towels, stored them in my closet at home, and took them out to admire them for years until I had proven to my mother that I could again grow my hair. (That's six years of staring at dead hair and wishing you could attach it to your head.)

I don't remember what happened when I walked into school the day after I got my haircut. I'm sure there were a lot of appalled faces. Very few girls had short hair at this point, so in that way I guess you could say I was a trendsetter. But no one wanted to play beauty shop with a girl who had short, layered hair, so my days of having "friends" via this game were short-lived.

Besides the fact that I could now use Short & Sassy

Shampoo (inspired by one of my childhood idols, Dorothy Hamill), not much good came out of the beauty shop game. I was being used for my hair, and because of my willingness to let girls mess with it, my hair went to the chopping block.

That should have been a lesson learned. But there would be more lessons. I won't go into them. You get the point, I hope. Wanting people to like you and doing whatever you can to get them to like you often leads to sadness. It can make you do things you never thought you'd do. It's not worth it.

So, there's this conundrum some people face. How do you act nicely toward others without losing sight of who you are?

It's actually pretty simple. You treat everyone the way you want to be treated, and if they start to treat you badly you walk away. Case closed. Also, easier said than done. But once I finally realized that I shouldn't hang around people who didn't treat me the way I wanted to be treated, I simply wasn't drawn to those types of people anymore.

Now, you might be thinking, "You said this life wasn't about you, but so far all you've talked about is yourself." Fair enough. That's because while I thought I was being really awesome to people, I was truly just concerned with getting them to like me. Once I realized that I didn't need to be doing that, it opened up a whole new opportunity for me to stop focusing on myself and be kind to others. And with that, you get the chance to understand how much joy you can bring into the world by concentrating on others, especially those who could really use your help.

Anytime you want to stop feeling sorry for yourself, volunteer at a food pantry. When you're sick of caring about why things aren't going the way you think they should, organize a clothing drive. Take the time to help out others and suddenly you will realize, "Wow, the world doesn't actually revolve around me. My happiness isn't the only thing that makes life great. Maybe I don't have that much to whine about." Don't just treat others the way you want to be treated; treat them the way they *should* be treated.

Life can be stinky for you sometimes, but it can be really unfair and stinky for other people. Make your life about making their lives better, and then you'll realize that this life isn't about you.

CHAPTER 3
USE COMMON SENSE—ALWAYS

My dad once said to me, "How can someone so smart have such little common sense?" That wasn't a harsh insult; it was the honest-to-goodness truth. Let's reflect on just a few times during my childhood and early adulthood that I threw common sense out the window.

On the last day of sixth grade, we got out of school early, but somehow I didn't know that. Of course, there are some very logical ways to handle such a situation. You could go to the office and ask to call your mother. You could ask a friend for a ride home. You could request to stay at school until your mother comes for you. (Keep in mind that we're talking about pre-cell phone days—okay, even pre-touch-tone phone days.)

I chose to start walking home.

This would not be such a big deal except for the fact that my house was 2.4 miles from the school, and I would have to walk along a two-lane highway frequented by 18-wheelers for part of the trip. Another reason that this didn't make any sense: *There was no reason for me to walk home.*

Why didn't I use one of the options listed above? I didn't want to bother the school secretary. I didn't want to bother the parents of any other sixth graders. I didn't want to bother the principal to ask if I could stay until my mother came. (Actually, I was intimidated by the principal, so walking 2.4 miles seemed much more appealing.)

I was about three-quarters of a mile into my journey, trying to look all cool and relaxed, when another mom—who had ten children of her own—slowed down beside me in her car and asked what I was doing. "Oh, I'm just walking toward my house," I said sheepishly. You can't fool a mom of ten kids. She knew I wasn't supposed to be walking home. "Get in the car. We're going to my house, and we'll call your mother."

Oh, my mother was thrilled to get that call. My child was wandering the streets instead of calling me for a ride? I don't remember the conversation on the ride home, but I'm pretty sure it had something to do with the need to boost my common sense.

Fast-forward a few years. I'm in high school. I'm a majorette. Our weekly practice with a choreographer is about a seven-mile drive from my house. I had a big-butt Chevy Impala, not the streamlined kind you see today. This thing was a boat. You practically needed a CDL to drive one. Also, it was not a newer model, so it had a lot of issues. Like, at one point the starter was acting up, and I had to use a broom handle to get it to work. And there were rust spots bigger than my hips on both ends of the rear bumper, so you could see straight through to the other side. It was not a pretty machine, but it usually got me where I needed to go.

I loved to drive other people places. It made me happy. (And, oh, lesson not learned, I also thought that saying "yes" to people would make them like me.) So when two girls on the majorette line called for a ride to practice one day, I was happy to oblige. Then two more called. And then . . . You see where this is going. It seemed like the entire majorette line of sixteen needed a ride to the other side of Youngstown that day. And guess who was too nice to turn any of them down? (You do see a pattern forming here, yes?)

Understand that this was 1981. We barely wore seatbelts in the front of the car, and who knew if they even made them for the back seats? We often sat three in a row across the front seat because the gear shift was on the steering wheel. Looking back, it wasn't all that smart, but it was parent-approved and that's how we rolled.

What was *not* parent-approved, at least not by my parents,

was piling a bunch of teenagers in a car to the point where the car is bulging at the seams. I think there were eight of us in the car, three in the front and five in the back. As big as this car was, it was not meant to hold eight people. And here is where the condition of the car comes into play. It did not seem to be very sturdy. All the main pieces felt like they were tied together with rope. Again, think of the era: Car inspections weren't required. Most cars were made of steel, not plastic, so rust was a common issue. The fact that it had nothing more than an AM radio was the least of my problems.

So take eight majorettes, throw them into an old car, and drive across Youngstown, Ohio. What could go wrong? Nothing, until you drive over a bumpy railroad crossing. Then, literally, the bottom falls out.

At first, it was easy to ignore the clunking sound coming from the back of the car. Just turn the AM radio up a little louder. But then the noise became like fifty tin cans attached to the back of a newlyweds' car. Soon, it got really hard to drive because, obviously, half of the parts underneath the car were dragging across the pavement.

And then things got smoky.

The smoke emanated from the back, but I was convinced the engine was about to blow. I flung the car into park and ordered everyone out. We were screaming and running and looking quite idiotic. The back of the car was smoking because the tailpipe and the muffler had been dislodged. Still, I was waiting for the entire car to explode like an old-fashioned mafia hit. (This *was* Youngstown after all.) We ran far enough away that the debris wouldn't strike us dead.

The damn thing never blew up; it just smoked for a long time. Eventually, I ordered everyone back into the car. We drove a mile or so to the choreographer's studio. A trim, narrow-shouldered, erudite man who probably had never done much more than pay someone else to replace the windshield wipers on his car, the choreographer hoisted the important parts underneath my car and tied them to the bumper with thick rope. The lesson then proceeded. I could put off the inevitable unpleasantness of telling my parents for a while.

I can't remember how we got home. Maybe my parents came in another car, or I drove the jalopy back home very carefully, still with the weight of eight people dragging it downward. What I do remember is not telling an exact truth to my parents.

"How fast were you going?"

Really slowly.

"How many girls were in the car?"

Five.

"How many?"

No, wait, six. No more than six because that's all the car can seat.

Liar, liar, your majorette uniform is on fire.

It took a year and a couple of beers at a tailgate during a college football game to spill the truth to my parents.

Remember that time when the bottom fell out of the Chevy? I had eight majorettes in the car.

"Do you think we're stupid? We knew you had too many girls in the car! We just can't figure out why you didn't use your common sense and tell some of them you couldn't give them a ride. You could have avoided the whole thing!"

I don't want to tell you how many times after that, in other situations, I thought to myself, "If you had used common sense, you wouldn't be in this mess."

Trust your common sense. It's like a wave of heightened awareness that comes over you when crucial decisions must be made. Should I buy this really expensive bracelet and max out my credit card, or should I save a little bit each month from my paycheck to pay for it? Should I give my number to this guy I only recently met? Should I loan money to this person even though I know she is not completely trustworthy?

I recently read an article in which the author spoke about the gifts of prudence and wisdom. Prudence means being cautious and not hasty so you can make the best choices.

Wisdom is the ability to see the bigger picture, from the past through the future, which allows you to guide others toward prudent decision-making. When you're younger, being prudent and wise sounds lame. As you get older, those become traits you strive to obtain. It wasn't prudent to drive an abundance of majorettes to practice. It would have been wise to think about the far-reaching implications of having too many people in the car would bring: putting other people in a potentially dangerous situation, forcing my parents to pay for expensive car repairs, and so on.

Common sense resides at the intersection of wisdom and prudence. While it can take years to fully grow, common sense is with you all the time, even as a youngster. You encounter common sense when you take a step back and think through a situation. The proper path may not be the one that is easiest or the most pleasant. It may not make you popular with others. It may take you way out of your comfort zone. But you'll be able to look back and congratulate yourself on choosing the approach that made the most sense and did the least damage.

CHAPTER 4
THERE ARE NO DUMB QUESTIONS, SO ASK AWAY

If there was anything I didn't want to do for a good chunk of my life, it was ask people questions. Why, you ask? (See, I told you there are no dumb questions.) Because I didn't want to appear like I didn't know what I was doing. Ah, but you're saying, how can you know what you're doing if you don't ask? Naturally, you sneakily pretend like you know what you're doing so it looks like you don't need any assistance.

The Internet of Things has alleviated some of the burden for those too chicken to ask for help or clarification. Not sure what your boss meant by those recent instructions? Just Google it and—voila!—you'll know what to do without seeming like an oaf to your boss. This doesn't mean, however, that you can Google your way into figuring out everything. It's important to let people know that you're interested enough in a situation to get all the information you need. This rather obvious notion seemed less-than-obvious to me as a young professional.

Case in point (and, by the way, it's very painful to go back to this memory): my fiasco first assignment at my first job out of college. Let me start by saying that I had been dreaming of working for a magazine in New York City since I was about 12 years old. I loved the energy of the city, and I craved the chaotic glamour that surely came with being a magazine journalist.

I took a job out of college with a major women's magazine. It was quite a privilege to be working for one of the "7 Sisters," as the top women's magazines of the time were known. What a thrill to walk from my L-shaped studio apartment, which I shared with a college friend, across the then rather unkempt

Theater District to a high-rise office building on the East Side of Manhattan. All of the noise and the debris and the chaos swirled together for a cacophony of excitement that made this Ohioan swoon with glee.

To be truthful, my walk to work was the best part of that job. Once I got off the elevator and headed toward my cubicle, something inside of me always screamed, "RUN!" even though I never did. This was the heyday of "paying your dues," when being an assistant at a magazine included a special kind of hell for the uninitiated. Only the strongest— or the craziest—survived, and the veteran editors often watched with bemused delight as another wide-eyed novice crashed and burned and eventually left to work for a small newspaper near their hometown.

This was not going to be me, of course. I had planted my feet firmly on New York City asphalt, and I wasn't budging. The only thing that would keep me from succeeding at this magazine would be my acute shyness, coupled with my uncontrollable fear of asking questions. Still, I pushed through, getting the executive editor's coffee and lunch orders, answering the phone and reading through unsolicited article queries that ranged from fascinating to freaking ridiculous. I carried all of this out while I secretly (or maybe not-so-secretly) trembled inside when my boss, the executive editor, or her boss, the editor-in-chief, came within 10 feet of my cubicle.

All I needed was to hear my boss berate me in her British accent, and I would collapse like a wet noodle. Even if she was bashing me for ordering the wrong type of salami on her sandwich—which she did on more than one occasion—and I stood up for myself—because I'm Italian and I thought salami was salami—I would be left shaking from head to toe.

I wasn't the only one feeling constant dread. A fellow assistant editor complained of constant pain in her thighs from the anticipation of having to leap from her seat to carry out orders from the higher-ups. One of the associate editors twisted a curl in his hair all day long as he worried that he might be summoned to the executive editor's desk for a chewing out.

For me, survival meant following a very tight plan:

· Go to work
· Do your job to the best of your ability
· Get yelled at for something relatively minor
· Get flustered and do something else wrong so you can get yelled at again
· Go back to your desk and finish your work
· Go home and cry yourself to sleep
· Repeat

Why stay, you ask? Because this was part of being a newbie at a New York magazine! Everyone made dirt money, worked hard for little or no recognition unless they did something incorrectly, and waited for their chance to move up. Some moved up more quickly than others, and those were the people who either had a family member in the business (and therefore could sidestep the more humiliating aspects of the job) or had been born with such a high level of confidence that even the meanest editor felt a sense of awe and reverence. I worked with one such person at this magazine. "Brenda" was only about two years older than I, but she was already being groomed for great things. The editor-in-chief *adored* her, and it was obvious to the rest of us.

Brenda didn't walk, she sashayed in a sophisticated way that said to the rest of us, "I'm richer than you, I'm smarter than you, and I will crush you if you even think about challenging me for an opportunity." I didn't have to look at the labels of her twill pants and cashmere sweater to know that one of her outfits cost more than my entire wardrobe. She was one of those people who, if you allowed yourself to buddy up to her, could possibly take pity on you and let you ride on her coattails. But I was way too insecure to try to match up with

Brenda, so I put in my time and hoped that eventually I'd get the chance to prove my worth.

I got a small chance to do just that when I was assigned the Coming Attractions blurbs at the back of the magazine. The Coming Attractions highlighted what would be featured in the following issue. Sounds simple enough. However, there is a certain way that a national magazine such as this one liked to have them written. You needed to look at back issues to get a feel for the wording and the style. You also needed to ask questions. For instance, "Is there anything especially significant about the upcoming articles that should be noted?" "Are there any words I should avoid?" What I have learned after all these years is that the more questions you ask, no matter how minute some may seem, the better the chances are of a successful outcome.

The managing editor of this magazine, who specifically told me to ask her if I had any questions, always seemed really busy, overworked, and stressed, so I chose not to bother her. The editor-in-chief, the person who would ultimately review the Coming Attractions, scared the bejesus out of me, and I would have rather swallowed a typewriter ribbon than ask her a single question. I also didn't really want to talk to her. So when she was at lunch, I asked her secretary if I could leave something in her office. I printed out the Coming Attractions and I left them *on her chair.*

I look back now and I think, "What the hell were you thinking? You leave things on chairs only for people you know well enough and who aren't several rungs above you in the office, people who won't feel that leaving work on their chair is disgusting because it's where they put their butts." I look back and I think that placing my work on the same place this lady put her butt was one of the worst things I could have done. Coupled with the fact that I did not produce particularly quality copy for her to review, it's no wonder things ended up as they did. I can laugh now—sort of—but I will do everything in my power to help you avoid a similar situation.

I went back to my desk and started typing or whatever, and about a half-hour later, the editor's secretary called me. She used her "I'm speaking quietly and solemnly to indicate to you that there is some unfortunate trouble headed your way" voice. She told me the editor wanted to see me.

Had this been 1997, I probably would have been chanting "DEAD MAN WALKING!" under my breath. There was no doubt in my mind I was going to an execution of sorts. When I sat down across from the editor's desk, she whipped around in her chair to face me, shaking the paper in my face.

"What is this?" she asked.

Her eyes—I can't remember if they were actually blue or green, but at this point they were bright red, and they almost burned me with their intensity. Her nose, which had a pronounced curve at the tip, stared down at me like the shiny barrel of a gun. At any moment, I expected that thing to start shooting rubber bullets at my face. All of this is to say, the woman was not happy with what I had presented to her.

"It's, um, the Coming Attractions," said I, innocently.

"I know what it is!" she hissed. Now her eyes appeared to be shooting daggers at me.

Honestly, at that point I must have confirmed to her that I was the biggest ass on the planet. Of course she knew what it was; she was asking why in the hell I thought they were ready to be viewed by the editor. I can't remember the actual writing on the paper, but I'm willing to bet it was not up to snuff for a national publication. Or maybe it wasn't that bad, but she was sore because I had placed it on her chair. Maybe she even sat on it before she realized it was there.

"I know what it is!" she hissed again, and this time, she tossed the paper onto her desk. I watched it float slowly downward, the same direction my young career seemed to be heading.

"How could you turn in something like this? What would possess you to give this to me without having someone else look at it first?" She slapped my Coming Attractions on her desk over and over until it resembled a crumpled paper airplane. On and on she droned. And then, when she ran out of ways to ask the same question, she took a different tack.

"You know who's a good writer?" Uh-oh, I thought, here it comes. "Brenda!" Yup, I knew it.

"Brenda could come in here and write these with her eyes closed, and they'd be great." Of course they would be; Brenda is the greatest thing since sliced bread, and I am just a crumb, unworthy of being on the same plate as mighty Brenda. Well, that's how I felt. I was too shy to stick up for myself, and too petrified to run out of the room. So I just sat there, motionless, my head absorbing all the tears I wanted to pour onto this woman's desk.

The editor picked up the pathetic piece of drivel I had written, the mangled piece of paper that seemed to represent my career in magazines, and railed at me again. "*Brenda* is the kind of writer we need. If you can't write like *Brenda*, there's no place for you here. Now I have to give these to *Brenda* so she can fix them."

Brenda, Brenda, Brenda.

If there had been an opening for me to say, "I'm so sorry, would you mind taking just a minute or two to show me how I failed?" I don't think I would have been able to get the words out of my mouth. Every bit of concentration I had was focused on not bursting into tears in front of this woman. I just wanted to get the heck out of there and back to the safety of my crappy little cubicle. And still, the berating continued.

Let me paint a bit of a picture to let you know how I felt. There is an episode of the classic cartoon show *The Flintstones* in which Fred is sitting in Mr. Slate's office getting reamed for something he did wrong. As his boss yells and belittles him, the big stone chair in which Fred is sitting gets bigger and bigger as Fred gets smaller and smaller. Eventually, the chair is huge and Fred is this little figurine that jumps from the giant chair and shuffles out of the room, dejected and humiliated.

At that moment in the editor-in-chief's office, I was Fred Flintstone. I distinctly remember, as she was rambling on about how I'd never make it in the magazine business, that I was indeed shrinking, and the wing chair in which I sat was slowly growing. "I am Fred Flintstone," I thought to myself. I remember leaping from the now seemingly huge chair and walking purposefully past her secretary and several cubicles of assistant and associate editors, all of whom craned their necks around their cubes so they could catch a glimpse of me. Their intent wasn't to mock me but to empathize with me. Many of them had done a similar walk of shame, or had at least come close. They nodded their heads in solidarity. "We understand. We are here for you." And more than a few were probably also thinking, "Thank God it wasn't me this time."

You could say, "What a mean woman to ridicule you like that." Remember, I did say I was terrified of this lady, and now you can see why. However, do not throw me a pity party. I set myself up for the humiliation. By being scared to ask the managing editor for her advice on how to write the assignment, and instead, tossing the copy on the editor-in-chief's chair rather than handing it to her and telling her that I'd greatly appreciate learning from her editing talents, I portrayed myself as someone who didn't care enough to do the best possible job. I certainly didn't come off as someone who expected to one day be a top-level editor at a national magazine. I was certainly no Brenda.

Although I may not have deserved the verbal thrashing I got, I did deserve a wake-up call. If you want to give the impression that you give a darn about schoolwork or your job or your relationships, speak up. Ask questions. Be sure that you are on the same page with others. You could even make *suggestions to do something differently and possibly even better.*

I will admit that sometimes my mind is blank. I'm not kidding. Not when I'm interviewing someone for an article, but when someone is talking to me for the first time in a social setting. Many people are able to rattle off questions with barely any time for responses. All I hear is rattling inside my brain.

After all these years, I've learned there's a name for my plight: selective mutism. Primarily a childhood issue, adults can sometimes have it, too. In my case, I probably had it as a child and carried it with me into adulthood. With selective mutism, a person who converses normally in most situations will suddenly freeze and be incapable of speaking when he or she is in an unfamiliar or uncomfortable setting. This peculiar issue has happened to me when I'm at a party, when I'm in a large group of people and expected to speak, or when I'm in a situation where I need to defend myself.

A 2015 study titled "Lost Voices and Unlived Lives: Exploring adults' experiences with selective mutism using interpretive phenomenal analysis" captured the experiences of five adults with selective mutism. One of them hit the nail on the head for me: "It's like that scene from *A Christmas Carol* where Scrooge looks through the window and he can see people having fun being together. I'll always be stuck outside looking in."

Of course, in the example above, I wasn't worried about not having fun; I was worried about not looking like a moron. But I have been in that person's shoes, looking in at everyone else acting so at ease and normal while I think about how to evaporate into thin air. It's important to realize that this happens. That doesn't make it any better, but you can teach yourself some techniques so you'll be prepared the next time it strikes.

Then there are times when I'm simply afraid to ask questions. "You'll sound like an idiot." "That's not a pertinent question." "What if everybody else knows the answer?" Have you ever felt your head swimming with these thoughts as you contemplate asking a question? They *flood* my brain all the time. Even now, it takes a lot for me to drown them out. But that is just what you've got to do. Because, although it seems counterintuitive, asking questions actually makes you look smarter, and it makes you look like you care.

CHAPTER 5

NEVER GIVE UP ON YOUR VALUES

Truthfully, holding onto your values and beliefs might not always be easy. Social media makes it especially hard. When I was growing up, we didn't have hundreds of thousands of strangers telling us how we should think and behave. We had our parents, our grandparents, our nosy neighbors, and a select close-knit group that wasn't afraid to say, "Do the right thing." Now, with communities larger than they used to be, families living greater distances apart, and numerous social media outlets, it's an awful lot easier to lose perspective.

Your values, whatever they are, were instilled in you by your family members, your spiritual community, your neighborhood. They can be as obvious as treating everyone with kindness to taking care of the environment. These values shape not just who you are, but how you will view society and how society will view you.

So why do some people leave home and twist or even abandon the values they received in their formative years? Sometimes it's rebellion. You know: I'm so happy to be away from my controlling, overbearing, and extremely nerdy family that I'm going to do things in the exact opposite way they taught me. It can also be peer pressure: Gee, Susie and Billy and Wanda are doing things this way, and they're telling me that it's okay, and they look like they're not going to fall into the fire pit of hell, so maybe it's okay for me to join them. Sometimes, we just feel like, "Okay, I've been doing things this way for eighteen years, and I'm not sure that this is really how things should be done, so I'm going to go over here for a little bit and see if the way they do it is better or more appealing."

And then sometimes, you can decide that your parents' values are whack. My parents didn't let me swear—at all. When I was really young, my dad didn't let me say "shoot" because it sounded too much like the other s-word. One time, I muttered "Jesus Christ" under my breath and my mother came at me like I had just attempted to set the house on fire. (For what it's worth, I am a firm believer in not taking the Lord's name in vain, but I was having one of those teenage moments and I just blurted it out like it was nothing.) By the time I was in my early twenties, I was swearing up a storm. D-words, s-words, f-bombs. It was what people did when they were talking to their friends or complaining about work. It felt *cool*, and who doesn't want to be cool?

Which leads me to this takeaway: At some point later in your life, you may very well realize that the childhood values you tossed aside are the ones that now make total sense. I don't swear like I used to (although I can still drop some great ones when I'm stuck in traffic). I think that the values my parents taught me make sense as an overall approach to living my best life and being good to those around me. Some of the values never actually left me; others I had put in limbo while I navigated my way through early adulthood. I wish I had never abandoned most of them because they were part of my identity.

If you stick to your values, you will sometimes be seen as nerdy. If you share them on social media, you may be in for some takedowns by people you don't even know. So, here's my advice: Keep your values close to your heart. It's not as important to voice them as it is to *live them*. People will know your vales when you act on them.

These days, it can feel like we've reached a saturation point when it comes to values. "I don't need to learn anything else, thank you. I know everything I need to live a great life." And then one day you're faced with something, and you're like, "Holy heck, I don't know how to handle this situation." This is either where your values will kick into high gear, or you will notice that your values didn't stick in the first place.

When I moved to New York in the fall of 1986, I basically had two nickels to my name. I had recently gotten my first job, with the national magazine. My college friend and I had just leased an apartment in Manhattan. Money was really, really scarce.

I was a week or so away from payday, and I probably needed groceries or some life necessity, so my friend/roommate lent me $50. I was so grateful. Until I got my paycheck. Then, suddenly, I was walking past a slew of electronics stores in Midtown, when I thought, "I *need* a Walkman." (If you don't know what a Walkman is, ask someone over the age of forty.)

I remember that feeling, even after all this time. Not just the idea that it would be nice someday if I had a device that would allow me to listen to the radio and CDs while I walked to work, but the strong, impulsive feeling that if I purchased a Walkman *that day*, my life would be changed for the better.

A note about small electronics stores in Manhattan during the late-1980s: They were a rip-off. Lined with the latest in technology, they lured you in with promises of the lowest prices in town (but who was going to check to make sure that was the case?) and an overly friendly sales guy out front who was just waiting for some yokel like me to come along. It felt like a magnet luring you in and leading you directly to the cash register.

My paycheck money had been freshly deposited into my account. The idea that I needed to pay back my friend was definitely in my mind, but as I browsed the Walkman selection at a particular store, that feeling became more and more overshadowed by a sense that I had to have a Walkman.

At the same time that I was salivating over the latest technology, I felt something nagging at me, a feeling pulling at a place inside of me that was so deep that it could only be described as my soul. That feeling, of course, was my conscience. Why would you ever not listen to your conscience? Well, when you've convinced yourself that you not only want and need something, you *deserve* it, that's pretty much when you stop listening.

I struggled to suppress my conscience as I ran my fingers along the newest and shiniest portable devices. Each one promised to transform my listening pleasure and, thus, my life. My conscience managed to turn me toward the door a couple of times, but the intuitive salesman drew me back with a lower price on one of the nicest machines. Finally, as I stood at the counter with my finger over my lips, desperately trying to decide if I should take out my wallet or run out of the store and never look back, the salesman went in for the kill. He offered me a price I couldn't refuse: $50.

Fifty bucks. The exact amount of money I owed my friend. Here was the ultimate moral debate! Do I make a beeline for the exit or hand over my money? Ultimately, an answer emerged: You'll get paid again in two weeks, and then you can pay back your friend.

Even as my conscience was throwing red flags in my face, I submitted to the lure of something new. After paying, I grabbed my Walkman—which came with free batteries and free headphones, so quite the deal—and headed out the door.

Later that day, I met up with my friend as we were heading out for the evening. We hopped into a cab and as we headed down toward Lower Manhattan, I revealed the joyous news. "Oh! Today, I bought a Walkman for $50. I'm so excited!"

I don't remember what she said, but she certainly didn't tell me off like she very well could have. I had just spent the money I owed her, and I made no mention of when I was going to pay her back. I'm fairly certain I paid her back as soon as I got my next paycheck, but that Walkman was forever stained with my greed and selfishness.

It's amazing to me that I still remember that incident. I see the details so clearly in my mind. Sometimes, if I allow myself, I still feel the wave of guilt that came over me. All these years later, it remains a shameful moment for me.

Small, insignificant story, right? Not if you think about how I was raised. You didn't borrow from someone and then get something for yourself before paying them back. It feels like a biblical lesson that would end with the borrower turning into a pillar of salt or some such punishment. I knew better. My values had been given to me at an early age, and I should have respected them. But the desire for a possession overpowered a sense of decency.

Everyone makes mistakes, right? Why beat yourself up about something that happened years ago? Because it is a painful reminder of how easily our values can be replaced by other things. The fact that I have felt a sense of guilt all these years is proof that I was blessed with a keen sense of right and wrong, and I sometimes really do a bad job of doing what's right. Why is that? I have no idea, but it's a fact that doesn't fade with time. All I can do is try to be better.

Don't forget your values. If you forget them, and you feel your conscience tugging at you, don't resist the urge to listen. The values that were instilled in you were done so for a reason: so you'd be a decent person and make a positive impact on others. In the end, it feels much better to be a decent person than it does to be something else.

Keeping your values doesn't mean that you can get all high and mighty when someone appears to have lost theirs. If I had a nickel for every time I said, "Why is so-and-so doing that?" I'd have the red Porsche 944 I salivated over when I was in my twenties. Even if you aren't religious, you can get behind what Jesus said about this: "Why do you notice the splinter in your brother's eye, but do not perceive the wooden beam in your own eye?" (Matthew 7:3)

I love the imagery of some guy walking around with a two-by-four stuck in his eye while he's saying, "Look at Bill over there with a little fleck of wood in his eye. Here, help me hold up my beam so I can continue to trash Bill."

If I had a nickel for every time I did that, I'd have two

Porsches and an Aston Martin. Guilty as charged. Why is it so easy to look at the flaws of others? Probably because it's less painful to comment on what somebody else is doing than it is to fix our own issues. "I can see exactly why Bill is doing what he's doing, even with this plank in my eye. Of course, my life would be better without the plank, but it's really just easier to concentrate on Bill and his splinter."

It took me a long time to figure out the significance of the plank metaphor. It is not just that you've got a big issue with which you're not dealing. It's that the issue, combined with your keen ability to focus on other people's issues, weighs on you physically, mentally, and emotionally. While outwardly it seems to feel good to point out the flaws in others, inside you continuously feel like poop. You know for a fact that you've got your own trials, but you don't have the intestinal fortitude to fix them. Because it's hard. So you walk around with this heaviness that feels somehow less burdensome when you note someone else's wrongdoing.

When I say "you," I certainly am throwing myself into the mix. If I got rid of the plank I've been lugging around all these years, I might just be a size two. It's easier to project an image of having it all together instead of being fallible. But when we realize our own fallible nature, we actually become kinder toward others. "Oh, you have this little flaw? Well, let me show you the multitude of inaccuracies I possess. We'll nod and laugh and help each other be better people." Sounds so refreshing, right?

Know that recognizing your own shortcomings and being less judgmental of others is a value. It's one that's easier said than done, but it goes a long way toward creating a kinder world.

CHAPTER 6
DON'T LET A WEEK GO BY WITHOUT CALLING YOUR FAMILY

"Saying goodbye since 1969."

My father's go-to phrase every time my brother or I packed up our car after a visit home. My brother was the first to leave, for college in 1969. My parents had several more years with me still in the house, but they seemed to always be saying goodbye to one of us. And they didn't like it.

You probably won't realize how painful it is for your loved ones to see you leave until you have your own children. Then one day they'll grow up and move on, and you'll be spouting tears like a waterfall.

It's important to realize that your parents, grandparents, or whoever played a large role in raising you want you to succeed; they also want you to have great experiences. Some people are better than others at setting their kids free. Some pretend like they're good with it but wait until you're safely out of the driveway to have a breakdown. Still others never shed a tear, as far as you know, but instead encourage you to fly.

No matter which type of guardians yours are, know this: They want to hear from you. Even if you have nothing to say. Even if you're homesick out of your mind. Even if you're having the time of your life and you're worried they'll feel bad because you're not homesick. Whether you need advice or money, whether you think your parents will give you either of those things or encourage you to figure it out on your own. Even if you've been given the impression that your parents aren't that worried about where you are and what you're doing.

Even if they don't think they need to hear from you, they do.

You may remember your parents whining about driving you to practices across town or dragging you to a family event you didn't want to attend. They may have complained on a semi-frequent basis about how much your education or your extracurricular activities cost. Your mom may have groused about constantly doing laundry (guilty!), and your dad may have said that your cell phone bill was going to force him to take out a second mortgage.

Let's be real. Being a caregiver to a child is a lot of work, and sometimes it's not fun at all. You may look at what your parents are doing for you and how they're reacting and think they're really despising this parenthood thing. Keep in mind that even those who grouse a lot (guilty!) wouldn't trade the experience for anything in the world.

Most of the time, being a parent is the greatest gift ever given. In what other role are you constantly solving problems, managing schedules, budgeting accounts, offering advice, building literacy and other empowering skills, kissing boo-boos, doling out punishments, rationalizing irrational behavior, wiping tears, giving unlimited hugs, and cheering on minor and major accomplishments, all with the objective of releasing a decent, well-rounded, success-minded and kind individual into the world?

And that's why it's so hard to let go.

You've helped this young creature along for a dozen-and-a-half years or more, with the intended goal of one day setting them free. And then when it's time to set them free, even if you know it's the right thing to do, it pulls a large chunk of who you are as a parent away from you.

"Thanks for the guilt trip, lady," you're thinking.

"You're welcome," I reply.

Because I had the same guilt trip every time my father stood near my car and sprayed it with his tears. I felt the pangs of guilt every time my mother would hurry through the house doing last-minute things for me and acting like it was such a chore, when really it was her opportunity to be there for me just as she was when I lived under her roof. The sense of remorse grew more distant the farther my car got from the homestead, but it continued to instill in me the idea that I was connected to my parents not just by birth, but also by spirit and emotion. You can cut the apron strings, but you can't cut the bond that is inextricably part of who you are.

That feeling kicked into high gear years ago when I'd be out with my friends in New York. Specifically, we would go to a local bar with a fantastic jukebox, and I'd play some old Sinatra song and call my parents, probably collect. (In pre-cell phone days, calling collect meant the person on the other end had to accept the call and then pay for it, usually based on a per-minute charge. So you knew someone really loved you when they told the operator they agreed to take the call.) The song would be playing in the background, and I'd be yelling into the phone about how the song reminded me of them. To my parents, it really didn't matter when I called, it was the act of calling that let them know I missed them and wanted to hear their voices.

Life will make you very busy as you get older. *You are never too busy to call your parents, guardians, caregivers—whoever it is that you call family.* Wait, modern child! You can actually *text your parents.* That's okay, too! Anything to let them know that you are out there and thinking about them. Because believe me, they are thinking about you. They might be at work, in front of the TV, at Starbucks, or drifting off to sleep. You are a part of their every thought. And they will be glad to hear from you, even if you are at a loud bar and they've been asleep for three hours. Well, maybe a text is okay in that instance.

The good news is that you can never contact your parents at a bad time. You can, however, wait too long to reach out, and that's when life can get a little unpleasant for you.

Here are some really great responses from my parents when

I had failed to call in a timely fashion (i.e., within five days of our last conversation):

"What am I doing? Sitting around waiting for you to finally call."

"Oh. What do you want?"

"Well, it's about time."

"Who is this?"

And my all-time favorite from my dad:

"Big deal."

Perhaps your parents aren't the king and queen of professional guilting like mine, but don't kid yourself that your parents don't want to hear from you. Or that they don't feel bad when you don't stay in touch. If you're blessed to have even a decent relationship with your mom and dad, you owe it to them to touch base. You owe it to yourself, too.

At some point, the relationship between offspring and parents shifts. The connection is no less significant, but it is far more equal. As you grow into adulthood, you (hopefully) reach a maturity level that allows you to become a more active participant in the world around you. It is also around this time that you (hopefully) realize your parents were not total dopes. In fact, you may find they're actually wise and even engaging. This newfound respect for your parents may lead you to new types of conversations where you are on an even playing field with your mom or dad. Your conversations may actually be—wait for it—fun.

Pardon the sarcasm. Just about every parent has experienced the feeling that their children don't look at them as humans. They are seen as taxis, ATMs, washers and dryers, grocery stores. They provide a lot of the comforts of life. Sometimes, we feel more like machines than people.

There have been moments when my bum was in the car for so long driving kids from one activity to the next, it felt like it had melded into the leather upholstery. No need to get out of the vehicle; just leave me in my upright position so I'm ready to roll the next day. We often move on automatic pilot. Time to make lunches, time to drive to practice, time to help with homework. As you get older, the tasks may be fewer, but they are no less taxing, and in a lot of ways they are more emotional: time to pick up the homecoming corsage, time to research geometry tutors, time to go on college tours.

Then the tasks come fewer and farther between and something miraculous happens. We start to feel less like machines and more like people. And guess what? We start to look human again to you! Meanwhile, as parents we see our kids as fully formed, hopefully mature, young adults who may not share our tastes in food, music, or movies, but who have smart opinions to explain their standards. And we, as the old fogey parents, may seem to have developed patience and a sense of humor.

And this is why you call your parents on a regular basis. Because they like talking to you and, gosh darn it, you kind of like talking to them. They're not looking for a laundry list of everything you've done since the last phone call—although they will gladly drink it all in if you choose to offer it. What you will find as you get older is that you can discuss all kinds of issues with your parents, and you can discuss them as you would with friends and colleagues (maybe not using the exact same language). And while this may seem like ordinary banter, very run-of-the-mill and nothing earth-shattering, it will mean the world to your parents—and to you. The bond you have with your loved ones may strengthen, or you may even find you've built a bond that before didn't exist. All because you picked up the phone and had a conversation.

Also, no one needs the parent guilt trip. So, if you start thinking to yourself, "I wonder if it's been a while since I called my parents," it probably has. Pick up the phone and say hello.

CHAPTER 7
KNOCK OFF THE DAYDREAMING

Listen, I'm not here to be the dream-killer. You'll see in the next chapter that I'm a firm believer in having a vision for the future and not letting anyone talk you out of it. But let's be real. There is a monumental difference between a vision and a daydream. Visions are the accomplishments you desire for yourself, and they require small milestones along the way to accomplish them. You want to be a photographer? Then you start taking classes as a child, get involved in photography in high school, and study at a college where you can get the best experience. You learn, network, and refine your skills, gradually leading to a future in photography.

Daydreams are those scenarios you create for yourself while you're driving your car or trying to make it through a boring lecture. You're not planning how you can get to a certain level; you're already there. It's as if you snapped your fingers, and suddenly you were photographing celebrities for *Rolling Stone* or faraway places for *National Geographic*. In your daydreams, you are amazing, even if you have no idea how you got there.

Daydreams can be fun. They kill time. They're very creative. But if you don't have a plan in mind to get to that daydream, it ain't gonna happen. At some point, the daydream becomes unattainable, although you may continue with the daydream because it feels quite pleasant and satisfying, if only in an imaginary way.

When I was a kid, I wanted to be a Rockette. Every Thanksgiving Day, I'd sit through the Macy's Parade waiting for that glorious moment when those beautiful, elegant dancers would do their number prior to Santa's arrival. I can still see them dancing around with Styrofoam candy canes, tap dancing their beautiful hearts out. You knew the end of the routine was near when the Rockettes would flap into a long, straight line and put their arms around each other. And then they would kick, in unison, not a single leg higher or lower than the other. The whole time, they would have amazingly wide and bright smiles, as if it was effortless to create such a seamless kick line.

Every year, immediately after the parade, I would dance around my parents' living room, shuffle-ball-changing across the floor, smiling like my mom had put Vaseline on my teeth, working myself into a fantastic frenzy until the grand finale. And I would kick like no one had ever kicked before, and follow that with a gracious bow.

And then I would stuff my face with mashed potatoes and gravy.

Long after Thanksgiving, I would imagine myself as a Rockette, doing show after show at Radio City Music Hall. During my weekly tap and jazz lessons, I'd pretend I was on stage, kicking up my heels to the sound of riotous applause.

What I lacked for this daydream to be realized was a clear plan. *I hadn't set any goals.* How was I going to get from Point A to Point B? What should my first step be? When you're lost in daydreaming, you don't worry about planning. You reach Point B miraculously. You just automatically are that talented and motivated.

As the years passed, I still imagined myself as a Rockette, although I was pretty much in the same spot in life. I was a chubby teenager instead of a chubby adolescent. I still danced a couple of days a week, and I was pretty good, but I wasn't pushing myself to be my best. I kept my daydream to myself so that no one had the opportunity to offer advice.

When I was a senior in high school, I went on a group trip to New York City. The tour included a visit to Radio City Music Hall. Imagine my elation, to be near the front of the stage where the Rockettes performed for throngs of people. I listened intently as the tour guide talked about the wonderful shows that took place inside the hall.

Then she focused on the Rockettes themselves. I was mesmerized. "They practice very hard, every day," the tour guide said. "They tour around the world," she added. "They don't make a lot of money at all," she then threw in. "Most of them have to have second jobs in order to live."

Wait. So my daydream vocation was a lot of work with very little pay? While this news shook me to my core, it eventually provided me much relief. Since I had never figured out a way to work toward becoming a Rockette, I had actually saved myself a lot of financial distress. In the end, I really did myself a favor.

Actually, I didn't. If I had really focused on becoming a Rockette, if I had put in the necessary practice time, done my research and ensured I was in top physical condition, I still likely wouldn't have made the cut. What I would have given myself, however, was the ability to set tangible goals along the way, and to at least make myself a viable candidate for something I so dearly craved. Instead, I had a lot of really neat "memories" from long daydreams of me wearing a sparkly leotard and high heels.

Contrast that daydream with my vision of attending Penn State. I knew since I was 11 years old that I wanted to attend PSU, and I knew what I had to do in order to get there. Study hard, be involved in extracurriculars, get a good score on the ACT or SAT. When I received my acceptance letter, it almost seemed unreal. You mean, if I actually create a plan and stick to it, I have a great chance of achieving my end-goal? What a concept.

It took a long while—I mean, a *long* while—to understand the difference between a vision and a daydream, and to realize that daydreams can be really detrimental to growth. If they fill a quick minute or two in your life—maybe when you're driving in the car and your favorite song comes on and for three minutes you're a rock and roll star on stage—that's pretty fun and really okay. If the daydream reaches epic proportions and takes up large chunks of your time, you've either got to stop daydreaming or get serious about trying to make that a reality.

Here's another danger with daydreams: They can keep you from being present. Instead, you're always envisioning the next great, perfect event or activity. You invent a world that is so flawless, you can't possibly enjoy the life you're really living. You can retreat to the daydream and make the real world more of a bother, something you have to do in order to get to the fantasy. Maybe you're struggling on the football field, and you start to imagine yourself playing in the NFL. Or maybe your first job is not as exciting as you had hoped, and so you create an ethereal realm where you're the lead photographer for a trendy fashion magazine or the top criminal lawyer in the country. Or maybe you're a good but not great dancer who continually imagines herself entertaining crowds in Manhattan. You get the picture. Don't let these fantasies get in the way of the life you should be living.

That's not to say that a daydream can't become a reality. If it seems viable, maybe you should cease fantasizing and commence with goal-setting. Maybe confide in someone to see if it's something that could be attained. Then comes the hard part: the follow-through. Once you've decided to try to make something happen, don't let doubt or laziness get in your way. Sure, it's much easier to daydream, but imagine the fulfillment of accomplishing what you set out to do. Imagine the confidence and satisfaction you could feel.

This leads me to another of my major daydreams. I have always wanted to learn to play the saxophone. In my daydreams I'm not just playing scales; I am in a big band on a New York City stage, as part of a modern-day, Glenn Miller-esque extravaganza. Never mind the fact that I have never so much as held a saxophone in my life. In my mind's eye, I am that good. What do I do with this daydream? Do I take it with me to my grave, or do I at least pick up the instrument and see if I can blow into it?

I have rather secretly guarded this daydream for years. Recently, though, I've kind of let it out of the bag, and it has not been received well. In fact, it's kind of become a joke. "Oh, listen, there's a saxophone in that song. Gee, Mom, maybe they should have called you to play?" Hardy har har. The only way to keep this joke from continuing is to finally get myself a saxophone. And that is what I'm promising you. I'm gifting myself with a beautiful sax very soon, and I'm going to learn to play that thing. And it may sound like tires screeching across wet pavement, and I'll probably never be invited to perform with a swing band. In the end, who cares? I will have finally—*finally*—taken that daydream out of my head and put into action. No matter what the outcome may be, I can only imagine the happiness I will feel for turning that daydream into a vision and that vision into some kind of reality.

CHAPTER 8
DON'T LET ANYONE TALK YOU OUT OF YOUR GOALS (AS LONG AS THEY MAKE SENSE)

In some instances, self-doubt can be the result of outside forces. My parents, God love them, had a saying they probably didn't even know they coined: "What do you want to do that for?"

I want to spend a semester in Italy.

"What do you want to do that for?"

I want to work in New York.

"What do you want to do that for?"

I want to move back to Ohio.

"What do you want to do that for?"

Every generation wants the next generation to fare even better. The problem is, sometimes the older generation doesn't quite grasp what that means. That may not be as true today, thanks to technological advances that give us a far greater appreciation for and understanding of the broader world around us, but when I was a kid it certainly was the case.

I come from a long line of people whose main reason for not trying something new is founded on fear of the unknown. What if you don't like going to college away from home? What if you get stranded in Italy with no way of ever getting back? What if you get abducted in New York? What if you move back to Ohio and you realize you should have stayed in New York?

The doubts kept coming at me even as I got older. How are you going to survive as a freelancer? Since when does anyone want to travel to Australia? Don't you know that no one over the age of thirty rollerblades?

None of this is to disparage my relatives. It was simply

not in them to entertain ideas outside of what they considered to be the norm. I give them enormous amounts of credit for eventually acquiescing to my constant badgering and begrudgingly accepting my wishes. I know that, at least after the fact, they were proud of my accomplishments.

So what are your goals? What do you see yourself doing five years from now? Ten years from now? Where do you see yourself studying, living, vacationing? What is the difference you believe you can make in the world? Are these goals attainable? Do they have the potential to better your life and those around you? Do you have a plan for making them happen?

Once you have the goals in mind, get to work on making them happen. Don't let my Rockettes story—which, if you're skipping around and haven't yet read Chapter 7, deals with goals that work out perfectly when daydreaming but stall when you never put a plan into action—discourage you. Instead, be inspired by the fact that I was fortunate to have done a lot of neat things, including working and living in New York City; traveling to Australia *twice;* setting up a pretty successful freelance writing business in Cleveland. Some of this was done with the support of others; some was not. All were accomplished with me having a burning desire to do something and then getting it done, despite what others might have thought.

The challenge with convincing others to embrace your goals is keeping them on board when things take a different direction. My parents had spent a decade trying to deal with the fact that I was living in New York. When I announced I was ready to move back to Ohio, I thought they'd be overjoyed. Instead, they were skeptical.

"Why do you want to move back *now?*"

"What if you miss New York after you leave?"

"How can you move with no real plan? No one does that."

I successfully got them to see things my way by giving them mature answers:

I want to move back now because New York doesn't have the

same energy to me that it used to. Plus, believe it or not, I really want to be closer to my family.

If I miss New York that much, I can always move back, or at least visit.

Actually, I moved to New York without a real plan. I'm moving back with the plan of being a freelance writer.

Eventually, everyone was on board with my move back to Ohio. Even the people at my office in New York understood, and they offered me an opportunity to freelance for the magazine. Things were actually coming together. Back home, my parents happily announced the return of their long lost daughter (who, in reality, had been home for a visit a month prior).

How was I supposed to get my stuff and myself from my apartment in New Jersey to my brother and sister-in-law's house in a suburb south of Cleveland? There was only one way: renting a truck. And there was only one driver: me. I couldn't find a friend to drive with me and then fly back, so I was going to do it solo. Truck drivers did it all the time. What's the big deal?

"You can't do that," my parents took turns saying. "No one does that."

"How do you know no one does that? I see rental trucks on the road all the time," I shot back.

This back-and-forth went on for several days. Then, one afternoon, I got a call at work. It was my parents.

"Diane," my father said in his worried-dad voice, "your mother and I just drove 50 miles on Route 80, and we didn't see a single woman driving a truck."

"You did what?"

"We went for a drive into Pennsylvania because I wanted to see for myself. And there were no women driving trucks. You can't drive a truck."

I must say, I was impressed. My parents had abandoned the typical "what if something goes wrong even though we have no way of proving that" approach. Instead, they actually did some of their own research. A 50-mile road trip in their giant Mercury Grand Marquis with my mother riding shotgun and on the lookout for female truck drivers, showed they had ambition and were concerned enough for my safety that they went out to prove me wrong. And after driving on the interstate for a certain amount of time, they felt comfortable enough to return home and call me with the results.

"No women drive trucks. You can't drive one."

Of course, I did. I rented a 15-foot yellow truck, and my friends came the night before to help me pack it up and hitch my silver Subaru to the back. And on the morning of October 31, 1995, I made my way across New Jersey, Pennsylvania, and a sliver of Ohio to my new life.

It was a goal. Not only did I want to move back to Ohio, I wanted to start a freelance writing career, and I wanted to be independent and get myself there without the help of others. And I did it. Not being monsters, my parents were of course glad that I wasn't robbed or abducted or sent to meet my maker before my natural time, even if it did prove their theory wrong.

Because I had accomplished my move on my terms, I was able to move forward with confidence with the rest of my goal. I got a part-time proofreading job and started building my freelance portfolio. I moved out of my brother and sister-in-law's house in a matter of months and moved to a cool little neighborhood just east of the city. I didn't talk myself out of any aspect of my goal, and gradually it happened.

The thing is, my family wasn't wishing me bad luck. They always want what's best for me. But fear of the unknown made my goals seem like scary encounters. It's natural to have those feelings, but if you believe in something and you know that what you want to accomplish has the potential to bring about wonderful consequences, no one should stop you. If you have a plan, you can make your goals a reality.

And never forget, real women drive trucks.

CHAPTER 9
ALWAYS TAKE THE TIME
TO STRETCH

I don't have much else to say on the topic. Just know this: One day you will go to bed feeling like your spry self, and the next morning you will try to get out of bed but seriously wonder if someone is holding your back in a vice. I wish I had taken the time to stretch first thing in the morning and last thing in the evening. I'm convinced that I would not have a clicking sound in my back right now if I had. (Yeah, that's gross. Sorry, but if I have to scare you into taking care of yourself, then that's what I'm going to do.) This is the best health advice I can give you while you're young: Do your damn stretches.

CHAPTER 10
NEVER FORGET WHERE
YOU CAME FROM

You can never take the working class out of me. Not when I spent a college semester in Italy. Not when I went to work in New York. Certainly not when I moved to Cleveland to start a career as a freelance writer.

It's not that I ever tried. It's that I never realized how working class I was until I got older. Being the first generation to go to college, growing up surrounded by family members who toiled in the steel mills or on the railroad, living in a community where no one thought they were richer or poorer than their neighbor, shaped every aspect of my life. Incredible amounts of pride and humility came with being working class. You could look at anything made of steel—a car, a bridge, a swing set—and know that the material may have come from the area, could have been made with your grandfather's hands. At the same time, you realized your place in society—not well off but not poor—and that was okay. Being working class made you work harder; it made you closer with your family; it kept you grounded. Even though I would envision one day living in a fancy brownstone in Manhattan, I felt a greater kinship with the secretaries in the offices where I worked because we were cut from the same cloth.

Now, there is a challenge that comes with staying close to your roots. That happens if you find yourself moving into a different cultural or socioeconomic level, or if you have aspirations to do so. When you are working class and you want to move into the world of magazine publishing in New York City, you face some challenges. Even moving into a large city or a different part of the country might present some obstacles you didn't expect.

Examples:

1. When you are in a grocery store in Greenwich Village, and you tell your roommate that you're going to grab a buggy. And he looks at you funny and asks you to repeat what you just said, and again you say "buggy," and he has to balance himself against the windowed wall of the grocery store because he cannot stop laughing.

"Honey, we are not in Youngstown anymore. It's a *cart.*"

Embarrassing.

2. When you go to a nice Italian restaurant in Midtown Manhattan with some people you've only recently gotten to know, and you look at the dish brought to the table next to you and exclaim, "Oh! They have sewer pipes!" Everyone looks at you like you just announced that you weren't born but rather hatched from an egg found on the side of the road in Paducah, Kentucky.

"You know?" you say while wearing a really broad smile and looking for understanding in the eyes of others at the table. "It's the long, tube-shaped pasta with little ridges running down the sides."

More blank stares, until someone looks at the plate at the table next to you, throws back her head and lets out a little whelp. "You mean rigatoni!" And the rest of the table cracks up as your face turns the color of marinara sauce.

Well, no, I mean sewer pipes, but you won't catch me saying *that* again.

Embarrassing.

Here's how to handle these situations: *Don't be embarrassed.* Where you grew up is part of who you are. You will always find people who don't talk about their roots or who talk about them disparagingly. Don't be one of those people.

"Well, guess what, buddy, we call it a buggy in Youngstown. I don't know why, but that's what we do. So get over it."

"I think the term sewer pipes to describe rigatoni is adorable, and I wish more people would say it."

Of course, I said neither of these. I shut my trap and made a mental note to not ever say either again, unless I was back in the safety of Youngstown. And by the time I had been away for a few years, the colloquialism left me. A cart was a cart. Rigatoni was rigatoni. I had changed in order to embrace the world I now occupied.

Now, that's silly. I agree, shouting "Grab me a buggy!" in the middle of a New York grocery store might elicit some stares. You don't have to give up everything you're used to saying and doing, however. If these colloquialisms are part of the fabric of your life, why rip them apart and throw the remnants in the garbage? You don't have to change your way of talking, thinking, or acting if you don't want to.

The other thing is, when you come home to visit and you try to act all fancy, you're going to tick off some people close to you. Like the time I came home from New York for a short vacation and I kept saying "*pa-JAW-mas.*"

"Oh, look at these cute *pa-JAW-mas* I got in New York."

"Mom, have you washed my *pa-JAW-mas* yet?"

"I'll go shopping with you—just let me change out of my *pa-JAW-mas.*"

I mean, how many times can you actually refer to your nightclothes, anyway? At this point in my young adult life, I wanted to be sure I injected some classy pronunciations into my everyday conversations back home in Youngstown. I probably used some other words in a pseudo-fancy way, but I mostly recall going on and on and on about *pa-JAW-mas.*

Finally, my mother had had enough. She turned to me and said, "I don't know where you're from, but here we call them *pa-JAA-mas.*" In other words, "Listen, smarty pants, you may think you live in a really sophisticated city and try to say things in what you think is a really sophisticated way, but you're still a girl from Youngstown."

Indeed.

All parents want their children to have more advantages and a chance for even greater success than they had. This was especially true for immigrants who worked hard in steel mills and coal mines to provide for their children. What they don't want is for their kid to come home and poo-poo how they speak or dress or act and use big words or exaggerated pronunciations to make them feel small. Because you may not be trying to make your family feel small or embarrass them, but that in effect is what you are doing. At the very least, you could be annoying them, and no one wants to annoy their family. Okay, maybe their siblings, but not their parents.

Wherever you go in your life, at some point you will miss aspects of your roots that make you feel happy, secure and comforted. For the decade that I lived in New York, I bemoaned the fact that I could not find a Catholic church selling pierogi on Fridays—or any day. The memory of those potato-stuffed dough balls smothered in butter and onions was one of the most vivid memories I took with me when I left home. Just knowing that they could be found at a nearby church at home provided comfort and a sense of belonging. Not having them nearby as a young adult gave me the sense that I was a million miles from home.

It wasn't just ethnic edibles that symbolized where I was from; it was also a small-town atmosphere that kept everyone connected. It also kept everyone up in each other's business. When you leave home for a big city, you're pretty much ready to put that behind you. Would I miss a family friend chastising me for getting a perm when I was nineteen? ("Don't ever do that to your hair again," I vividly remember this woman saying, as though my tight curls offended God and man.) Heck, no, I wanted to be able to do what I wanted—even if it turned out to be a gargantuan mistake—without friends and family weighing in.

If you're like me, a time comes when you miss having people all up in your business. Whether it's just your family or a whole village of busybodies, even if they are giving you grief over something you really like, it's nice to know they *care*. It's important to remember that these people aren't trying to trash your life; rather, they're trying to enrich you. The family friend who basically said a perm made me look hideous was saying much more: You don't need to do something radical with your hair to feel special; just be who you are. Of course, it would have been much gentler had she actually used those words, but the sentiment was in the end the same.

You can move away from your roots—in fact, I encourage it. Step outside of your comfort zone. Move to a bigger city, a smaller town. Move from the north to the south or from the United States to the United Kingdom. But don't forget where you're from. Bring part of who you are to every place you visit. Learn from others and let them learn about you. Just don't forget to come back home.

CHAPTER 11
QUIT YOUR BELLYACHING

If I had a nickel for every time my father said this to me. Can you blame the guy for not having much sympathy for my whining? Here was a man who lived through the Great Depression, eating squirrels and other critters that scampered across the yard; served as an Army mess sergeant in Germany during World War II ("the only dummy who would volunteer to bring food to the front lines," as he always quipped); and endured a number of painful personal losses. And here was his daughter, ten years old, living in a comfortable ranch house, eating more than enough food to keep her healthy (and chunky), enjoying the modern conveniences of the time (which included color TV and air conditioning), and all she could do was pout over her crappy misfortunes.

Sure, there were some instances that merited a good cry. For the most part, though, I had it pretty easy. And yet, I would get so down on myself and my lot in life.

I could blame this on a lot of things. I grew up surrounded by older relatives and didn't have the usual kid experience of playing down the street with the neighborhood kids. Maybe when your next-door neighbors are your sexagenarian aunts and uncles and they're dealing with things like backaches and UTIs, it rubs off on you. Not only was I an old soul, I was a cranky old soul.

Whininess grates on people's nerves. Any whiner knows this. And so the plan of action is to whine even more. This will lead people to either appease you in order to get you to shut up or walk away from you in disgust. With my family members, it was usually the former. As you get older, though, you find more people will walk away when you refuse to stop complaining about how awful your un-awful life is.

I complained a lot in high school. I complained a lot in college. I complained a lot in my twenties. Are you seeing a pattern? I complained. If I didn't get the A I was looking for in Spanish, I got angry and pouted. If I didn't enjoy my walk across a windy campus to get to my class on Chaucer, I groused. When I was having a hard time connecting to my copy editor job at a magazine, I drank wine while I complained. The situations changed, but the attitude didn't. What the heck was my problem?

Sometimes, I'd see people inch away from me. "I'll save my sympathy for someone who's actually struggling," I'm sure some of them said to themselves. "I can't be with this Debbie Downer anymore," others likely muttered.

In all honesty, I didn't recognize my propensity for belly-aching until about six or seven years ago. Up until then, I was whining about stuff that really seemed high level to me at the time: being awakened in the middle of the night by one, two, or three children; working from home while trying to keep up with laundry, cleaning, dog care, and so on; driving in a once-reliable car that the children now referred to as a death trap.

Woe is me, right? How could anyone live under such awful conditions? Can't those kids just stay in their beds? Can't you hire a cleaning service to give you a break? Won't your husband see how debilitating it is for you to be driving a ten-year-old car?

Even in the midst of these sob stories, I knew that I was exhibiting misplaced crankiness. Some people weren't able to have children, and they'd give anything to be up in the middle of the night with a sick kid. Some people were unemployed and didn't have a place to live. Some people couldn't afford a car. I knew that I was upset about not reaching perfection, and that I had no right to do that because so many other folks had it much, much worse than I.

I can't pinpoint when I made the leap from bellyaching

to acting more grateful. I do know that I wish I had felt that a long time ago. I think about the roommates, the friends, the coworkers, the husband, and the parents who have had to put up with me. Most of them stuck around, thankfully, because apparently I had some redeemable virtues. Still, I think about the relationships that might have blossomed had I stopped thinking about myself for a while.

So that's it, then! Selfishness. I was so caught up in my own little world that I couldn't crawl out and see how good I actually had it. My empathy for others remained very much intact, but I still had to see everything through my own narrow lens.

Sometimes, I get really down on myself about this, but then I realize that I'm maturing. Yes, it's sad that I seem to be maturing just as my AARP card arrives in the mail. Maybe I was maturing, however slowly, all these years. I suppose it's better than regressing. I mean, what if I started out as a really happy-go-lucky, glass-half-full person and then with each decade I became a sourpuss who darkened everyone's doorstep with her negativity?

Man, that sounds really ugly. If you're already an upbeat person, don't let yourself drift into whiny behavior. If you share my past bellyaching ways, snap out of it! No one—and I mean, no one—likes to hear sob stories for no good reason. Of course, there are times when life is hard and, unfortunately, can even seem unbearable. Naturally, you want to reach out to loved ones for compassion, understanding, and guidance. In that case, don't hold it in.

One way that I've managed to keep griping without losing friends is by using humor. With this method, you make people laugh while you get out all of your angst.

For example:

Several years ago, I was getting ready to meet former coworkers for dinner. I was notoriously late for these events, and I was determined to get to this event on time. It was the middle of winter, and my husband was preparing to use the wood-burning fireplace. The first time smoke filtered into the living room, he should have stopped. But he was determined. So he kept trying to light a fire and have it successfully move up the chimney.

In the meantime, our four-year-old son had decided to misbehave, and this was no time for that, since my husband was hell-bent on proving his wilderness skills. He put the poor kid in a time out on the steps—as smoke seeped through the house.

I came flying downstairs as soon as the smoke alarm went off, and I almost tripped right over my own kid. "Honey, get upstairs! It's smoky down here."

"Dad says I have to stay here," he said, his eyes getting misty from the smoke."

Well, I grabbed that kid and put him upstairs with his sisters. And then I went down to give my husband a talking-to. He was so fixated on making this fireplace work that he was completely unaware how smoky the house was getting. He was coughing and wiping tears from his eyes, but he insisted that he had this under control.

And then the fire trucks came blaring down our street.

"Why are they here?" he shouted.

"Well, the house is basically filled with smoke," I replied.

"Who called them?"

"The smoke alarm is connected to the home security system, remember? And the security people automatically notify the fire department."

His eyes bulged with horror. "Well, go out there and tell them I've got it under control." With smoke swirling around him, he bore a resemblance to Pig Pen, the messy character in the *Peanuts* comic strip. Drops of sweat clung to his temples.

I shook my head, but I walked toward the front door. And there they were. Four firefighters with axes in hand, ready to break down our door if necessary.

"They're here," I called in a sing-song voice to my husband.

"What!" he shrieked. "Tell them to leave." My husband began to wave a wad of newspaper around the fireplace, as if this would cause all the smoke to dissipate before the firefighters arrived.

"Um, they're coming in," I said, as I unlatched the front door and greeted them.

So the house is filled with smoke, my husband is still trying to light small pieces of paper and throw them into the fireplace, the kids are upstairs begging to come downstairs, and I am now officially really late for my dinner with my former coworkers. Talk about unexpected surprises.

Several minutes later, the firemen successfully convinced my husband that there was something wrong with the flue of our fireplace and that he should stop trying to light a fire. We flung open all the windows and let the cold winter air diffuse the smoke. And the kids were calmed by treats and a video. My husband's pride was hurt, but our house was not. Eventually, it seemed okay for me to leave the premises.

The whole way to the restaurant, I kept wondering how I would apologize for my lateness. The easiest approach, I at first thought, would be to complain about how horrible my life was. Certainly, this wasn't an isolated incident. Awful things happened to me all the time, and it was no wonder that I was often so upset.

Then, it dawned on me: Who really wants to hear that spiel? Was that why we were getting together for dinner, to listen to me go on and on and on about my really terrible experience? That's when I decided to turn the story around. It actually was pretty humorous, in all of its ridiculousness. Why not try to make everyone laugh instead of being annoyed?

So I raced into the restaurant, and as soon as I saw my friends tapping their wrists to suggest how late I was, I sprang into self-deprecating humor mode. "Oh, do I have a story for you guys!" I yelled before I had even made it to the table. Suddenly, the looks changed from slightly annoyed to definitely curious. "This is going to be good!" one of them said. And it was. We were laughing almost the whole dinner over the fiasco from which I had just escaped.

Not only did laughing about that incident make my friends feel better, but it also made me feel better. Instead of wallowing in self-pity and questioning why something always had to happen every time I tried to leave the house (which I admit is an exaggeration), I thought about how lucky we were to not have had any serious issues and how slapstick the evening had actually been. To this day, my family looks back on that story and smiles.

Not that long ago, I viewed any negative situation as a sure sign that life was against me. When you dig yourself into this woe-is-me hole, it's extremely difficult to crawl your way out. Just as you begin to make progress, any minor setback will send you sliding to the depths of despair.

Sound dramatic? Consider this case in point:

Several years ago when I worked in New York City and lived in New Jersey, a Nor'easter swept in rather unexpectedly. Wikipedia defines a Nor'easter as "a macro-scale extratropical cyclone in the western North Atlantic Ocean . . . usually accompanied by very heavy rain or snow." Simply put: It is a ginormous storm that builds off the coast and throws around enormous amounts of wind and precipitation. This particular Nor'easter came into Manhattan like a wrecking ball, and it left with just as much fury.

So strong was a particular gust of wind and rain that it blew my eyeglasses off my face as I was stumbling toward the commuter train. I had no time to grab onto a stem of my glasses; the wind just whooshed past me and took my spectacles with it. I immediately panicked. My eyesight at the time was not what you would call 20/20. I relied on contacts or glasses to find my way around, especially to drive my car from the train station to my apartment.

The wind and rain were pounding at my head; commuters

were frantically trying to push their way through the storm to get to their trains or buses; and I was spinning around like a whirling dervish frantically trying to find my glasses. A kind passerby noticed me and, even in the midst of the storm turning his umbrella inside out three or four times in a matter of seconds, stopped to ask if I needed help. "Yes!" I yelled through the sound of the wind, pellets of heavy rain pounding on top of my head (I'm fairly certain I'd lost my umbrella earlier in my trek). "The wind blew off my glasses and I don't know where they are!" I probably was crying, but it was hard to tell with all the precipitation cascading across my face.

The kind gentleman did a quick look to his right and then to his left. "I'm so sorry. I don't see them!" he shouted. I couldn't blame him for his half-hearted attempt at helping me. The weather was awful, and he certainly was as desperate as I was to get to the train station and trudge home.

I spun around a few more times, hoping in some pathetic way that my glasses would just be lying on top of a garbage can or along the curb. After a minute or two, I gave up. And I fumbled my way to the train station.

When I got there, of course, the train for my stop wasn't working so I had to take a train to the other side of the town where I lived. I wasn't alone. There were about four or five of us, drenched rats, shivering and complaining about the unexpected deluge. Only I had the magnificent story of Mother Nature absconding with my glasses. A brief chorus of "wows" and "that stinks" followed, but soon even these folks had had it with my sob story and concentrated on how they were going to get home.

A few of us climbed into a cab, where we told the driver our adventure. He, too, was shocked but not overly sympathetic to my story. I'm not sure what I expected from people at this point. Maybe if just one of them had said, "Lady, you've got the worst luck ever," I might have felt better. Because that's certainly how I was feeling.

The cab driver dropped us off at the train station, which meant I had to drive a mile from there to my apartment. You never saw anyone drive so carefully in your life, and when I finally crawled into a parking space outside of my apartment, I rested my head against the steering wheel and started to sob.

Looking back, this was a great story. Not in the sense of it being a fortunate event. On the contrary, this was a most unpleasant incident. But the hilarity of the situation—my glasses lifting off my head without warning, me spinning around in the storm in a foolish attempt to find them, the snail's-pace drive from the train station to my apartment—could be told in such dramatic and vivid detail, that people couldn't help but laugh.

I didn't want to laugh, however. This, as far as I was concerned, was the latest in a slew of events that proved the world was out to get me. I could not catch a break. Nothing this awful ever happened to anyone else. Every time I thought I was doing well and moving along smoothly in my life, some horrendous catastrophe came along to knock me back down.

What a bunch of hooey! Did I really think I was walking around all my life with a target on my back? Yes, I did. Never mind that I had gotten a great education, I'd traveled, I was working in a city I loved, I had a lot of friends, and I was healthy. I simply had bad luck. Horrible luck. The kind of luck that could make a person feel like giving up. But give up from what? Life? Did I feel that things were so horrendous that there was no sense in continuing?

No way! I wanted to keep on living; I also wanted to keep on bitching about my circumstances. At the same time, I truly believed that I wasn't meant to be happy. And I wanted the world to know.

Looking back, if I had been one of my friends, I would have walked away. Who needs a Negative Nellie in their lives? How can everything be so ridiculously bad to someone who doesn't really have a bad life? At what point do you just cut your losses with a friendship and move on to happier people?

Well, I know why they didn't leave. Even through the mild hysteria and nauseating whining that I did, I was a decent person. I would do just about anything for my friends. I liked to make them laugh. The good outweighed the bad, thank goodness, and my friends stuck around.

I look back and wish that some of the people who were in my life then could see me now. It took a long time to get rid of the condition from which I suffered, and sometimes I still have setbacks. But I realize how fortunate I am. I understand that when it comes to bad luck, mine has been pretty mild. I recognize that the eyeglasses story can be used for comedic effect, which I've done on more than one occasion, and that people like it a lot better when you aren't trying to get them to feel sorry for you.

You may sometimes feel like the world has it out for you. You lose a document you've been working on for school and you've got less than two days to redo everything; someone you liked ends up liking someone else; your next-door neighbor hits a foul ball that lands through the windshield of your new car. Life can be stinky, and sometimes it smells like a garbage dump. It's important to remember during these times that unpleasant events don't define you. My life wasn't ruined because I lost my glasses in a storm. I had to buy a new pair of glasses—big deal!

Put things into perspective. A few strokes of tough luck aren't going to send you spiraling into a life of doom. If you keep thinking that way, though, you'll effectively create a negative aura that will be a real bummer for you and those around you.

What's that saying? When life gives you lemons, make lemonade? Okay, keep that in mind. Turn your negative into some really good lemonade. Do it quickly, before anyone sours on you.

Both of the stories I shared have two very important morals I hope you'll remember:

1. Don't throw yourself a pity party and expect everyone else to attend.

2. If you do have something to complain about, see if you can turn it into a good story. Laughing feels much better than whining.

CHAPTER 12
BRUSH YOUR TEETH

I know you will try to blow right past this chapter. Why is this old woman talking to me about teeth? This is not going to better my life.

Promise me that someday you'll come back and read this whole chapter, before you have a mouth full of dental work.

When I was in my early thirties, I went on a diet to lose the last bit of baby fat I had been carrying around since I was five. I had been reading about low-carb diets for years, but the thought of going on one appalled me. How in the world do you live without pizza and lasagna (and bagels and hot pretzels and cereal and . . .)? Still, it felt like giving up my most beloved foods would be necessary to shed some pounds. So I went on a low-carb diet.

While I eschewed most things made with flour, rice, and potatoes, I found I had to have a crutch to fall back on so I wouldn't die of food deprivation. (What a drama queen.) I found my salve in gummy anything. Gummy worms, gummy Lifesavers, Swedish fish, Twizzlers. Ahhh, I still get nostalgic thinking about the beautiful taste of sugar and artificial flavors that sated me between low-carb meals.

Of course, there are two problems with this:

1. Gummy bears and Twizzlers are actually *filled with carbs*, which defeated the purpose of a low-carb diet. It actually worked quite well for years; it seemed my body was able to tell the difference between sugar-carbs and flour-carbs, and I really did lose a lot of weight. But you can't sustain that type of diet forever, and by the time I turned forty, it was catching up with my waistline.

2. Sugar rots your teeth. This fact gets drilled into our heads at an early age, and still we don't pay attention. A diet full of sugar is going to eat away at your teeth. And, sure enough, about three years after I started these eating habits, I got the first cavity of my life. And then they just kept on coming. Every few trips to the dentist, a nasty little cavity would rear its ugly head.

I know what you're thinking: Sounds like brushing your teeth wasn't the real issue, but eating sugary foods was. Well, yes, I agree. So let me back up a little bit. Brush your teeth, but also don't eat too many sweets. A little candy here and there is no big deal. A lot of candy every day is really bad. Yes, I should have known this by the time I was in my thirties, but I was more focused on finding a way to lose weight and still satisfy my taste buds. I might as well have opened a box of sugar and rubbed it on my teeth. It would have had the same effect.

So, okay, don't eat too much sugar. But also don't forget to brush your teeth. One of the more appalling statements I've heard as a child leaves for a sleepover is this: No one brushes their teeth at a sleepover. (Apparently, no one brings a change of clothes either, which is why children arrive home in the same clothes they've been wearing for thirty-six hours.)

1. Ew.
2. How do you have any friends?
3. Do you want a mouthful of cavities by the time you're twenty-one?
4. Did you know that bad microbes make themselves at home on unbrushed teeth with a slimy, sticky material called matrix?
5. Do you hope to someday have a significant other?

I'm assuming that sleepovers also include ingesting large amounts of snacks, such as popcorn and candy. Those little bits of food are taking refuge in your teeth while you sleep. Gross. Naturally, you will come home and brush your teeth (eventually), but a lot of damage has already been done.

"I'm not a toddler," you're saying to yourself right now. "Why are you giving me instructions on something I've known for years?" Because I was in my thirties and eating sugar like it was at the base of the food pyramid. At that point in my life, I had been a professional living on my own for ten years. Apparently, I still needed reminders about how to keep teeth free from decay.

Roll your eyes if you will. Consider this a public service announcement with long-term benefits. Keep your teeth clean and white, so the microbes that were freeloading in your mouth will have to find another mouth to invade. You'll have fewer trips to the dentist. And possibly more admirers.

CHAPTER 13
LAUGH AND THE WORLD LAUGHS WITH YOU

If only we had SpongeBob when I was a kid. There's a chance many of us could have learned to laugh off our embarrassing, awkward moments.

In one of the more memorable episodes of this cartoon, SpongeBob goes to a beach in Bikini Bottom, where he splits his pants while lifting weights. His friends crack up, and SpongeBob realizes he can make people laugh through his goofy behavior. He keeps ripping his pants on purpose after that, and gets a load of laughs, until it becomes too much and the gig is retired. But what a gig it was. Making light of something embarrassing that happens to you is a great way to turn humiliation into a bonding moment. It could even lead to a song, as it did for SpongeBob:

"I thought I had everybody by my side,
But I went and blew it all sky high,
And now she won't even spare a passing glance
All just because I ripped my pants."

For a while, at least, SpongeBob is Mr. Popularity in Bikini Bottom.

How I wish I had taken that humorous approach at the Rollercade in Boardman, Ohio, in 1977 (give or take a year) when—yes—I split my pants.

Let's get right to the heart of the matter and admit that I had no business being on roller skates. I've always liked being in control of where my legs are going, and as a kid I never felt in control with wheels or blades strapped to my feet. While I could hold my own in a pair of tap shoes, I was less-than-steady in skates.

And we might as well add here that I was chubby in those days. This was before "fat shaming" was a thing. These were the days when Sears proudly sold its "husky" brand of pants, and I, for better or for worse, was one of their favorite customers.

I don't think I was obese. It wasn't like I could barely pull myself up from a chair. In fact, I took dance lessons and I was pretty mobile, but I liked food. I still like food. But back then I *really* liked food. I'm fairly certain I never said "no" to a dessert, unless it was the chocolate-covered cherries my great aunt used to bring to holiday celebrations.

(By the way, what's the shelf life of a chocolate-covered cherry?)

So, at age eleven, I was chubby. Husky, if you must. And I was one of those people who tried to be kind of quiet in the hopes that my shyness would balance my chubbiness. I was always trying to do things without exerting a lot of energy so that I wouldn't look like the Michelin Man when I was at a dance class or playing a sport in gym or roller skating at the Rollercade.

It was very hard for me to advance outside of the beginner circle at the Rollercade. That's because I didn't want to draw too much attention to myself, and I didn't want to flop on the wood floor and make a big splat. But at some point, you get a little too old for the beginner circle, and I had probably aged out a couple of years earlier. Plus, all my friends were in the advanced lanes, and it was getting pretty boring skating in a dizzyingly small circle with a bunch of first graders.

One evening, a friend of mine lured me out of the beginner circle so I could join people closer to my age. I was very cautious, always certain the next step was going to be my last. At the same time, I attempted to play it cool, like I was perfectly okay walking gingerly on wheels because that is just how cool people like me roller skated. Skater after skater whizzed past me as though this were some sort of roller derby race. What's the hurry? Take baby steps with me and we'll all be happy.

At some point in the evening, I got dragged into going faster. My friend offered to hold my hand for balance, but eventually she let go and I was rolling on my own. I felt like I was going faster and faster, and the wall that I so desperately needed to roll into in order to stop seemed miles away. Trying to act cool was now out of the question. I was completely out of control, with arms flailing and my legs kicking wildly beneath me. Spinning, sliding, and finally crashing, I came down like bowling pins impacted by a terrific strike.

Just get up, I told myself. *Get back on your feet and start skating again. Everyone falls.* Great advice, self. It is important to recover and get right back in there. Which is what I did, although I couldn't help noticing that there was an awful draft right behind me. I reached back ever-so-slowly, and to my horror, my hand made contact with my underwear.

I had split my jeans.

You will have moments like these, when instant death seems preferable to taking another breath. The humiliation was instant. There was no chance of acting cool now. In fact, the only thing that was cool was my butt. My (facial) cheeks burned with embarrassment. The palms of my hands appeared hot and red since I used them—in vain—to minimize my fall.

Don't ask me how I got out of the rink, but I do remember my father standing by the edge—in a pair of his checked pants and a monochromatic polo, his black hair peppered with flecks of gray framing his puppy-like hazel eyes—shaking his head, no doubt thinking, *Why is it always my kid?* I wanted to go home, immediately, sooner if possible. My father wouldn't hear of it. We had driven other kids to the rink, and he wasn't making all of them end their night of fun.

A kind employee rushed over with about a dozen safety pins. I like to think that she was so prepared because she had done this many times before. I couldn't have been the first person to rupture her pants while roller skating, could I?

The rest of the evening is insignificant. With my pants safety-pinned from front to back, and me worrying that if one of those pins popped, I might be in an incredible amount of pain in a very private place on my body, I made my way back to the beginner's circle, defeated.

Ah, but it could have been much different if I had learned to laugh at myself.

Imagine if I had dramatically splayed myself on the floor, feigning death? How about if I had gotten up quickly, turned to those behind me and taken a bow? What if I had convinced my father to strap on some skates and get out there with me, the two of us comically pulling on each other for support? I tend to think the whole place would have felt much better, not just me. I could have relished the fact that I had made people laugh because I *wanted* to make them laugh, and not because I had done something embarrassing.

Embarrassing events are bound to happen. You're going to make mistakes and look silly on at least one occasion. Laugh (when appropriate) and chances are you'll start feeling better immediately. You'll probably make people around you feel better, too, because you'll be eliminating the awkwardness they will face as they wonder how to respond.

CHAPTER 14
THERE IS NO TIMETABLE FOR PULLING IT ALL TOGETHER

This book gives sage advice for teenagers and young adults, but I hope you've noticed that there's a lot in it for you older and wiser folks as well. Many of the lessons I've learned happened later in my life, long after my so-called formative years when I was supposed to be figuring everything out.

Interestingly, I thought I was very mature in my teens and twenties, so the idea that I needed to learn some lessons didn't even occur to me. Now I realize just how much of a naïve fool I was. That's actually okay. While it may be a little uncomfortable to look back on what I've done that I wish I hadn't, these foibles reveal an imperfection that should be embraced.

It's okay to make some silly mistakes—some, not a lot—if they lead you toward a greater sense of maturity. In my case, that didn't always happen. Despite being humiliated by a magazine editor for turning in half-assed copy, I didn't learn to open my mouth and ask good questions until years later.

On the other hand, there were important lessons I inadvertently gleaned that would aid in my maturity and self-respect. That incident at the magazine, and several others that occurred at the hands of other editors at the same magazine, taught me what I would and would not tolerate in an employer. I was okay with being reprimanded for not doing a good job, but I would never again allow myself to be humiliated and belittled. And I vowed that if I was ever put in a managerial position, I would never treat anyone the way I had been treated.

Other lessons took longer to penetrate my brain. I didn't stop daydreaming until probably four years ago. I know, that's really pathetic! Not that I was still pretending I was a Rockette, but I continued to envision an ideal situation that was unattainable. Luckily for me, when I finally stopped daydreaming, I recognized the value of setting goals. Although some of my goals have taken longer than I'd hoped (this book was supposed to have been written six years ago, for example), I've also learned the importance of patience. If you want something to happen, if you work at it, and if it's meant to be, it will happen. You may not be eighteen or twenty-eight or even forty-eight when it happens, but it will happen.

Realizing that you were never as mature as you thought is humbling, but once you embrace it, you're ready to accept a new level of understanding about the world and your place inside of it. I probably was never going to be a Rockette. I accepted that a long time ago, but I still had regrets about not following a path as a dancer. Once I stopped beating myself up about that, I understood that the gifts I've been given were meant for other things, like writing and volunteering and raising my kids. Instead of getting down on myself for things that I thought I should have accomplished, I can look back at my younger self with a sense of amusement. All of the good, the bad, and the embarrassing weave a story of an imperfect person trying to find her place. It took about a half-century, but I'm just about there.

As I was writing this chapter, a post popped up on Facebook that made my heart stop. It was so conveniently intertwined with the theme of the chapter that it seemed to have been placed there just for me. The post quoted a section of the book *A Year of Miracles: Daily Devotions and Reflections* by Marianne Williamson, an author, a spiritual leader, and (briefly) a candidate for the 2020 Democratic presidential nomination. I've found a lot of what she says to be "out there," but also some of it to be spot-on. In this case, her words were a direct hit.

In the chapter "On Life as a Spiral," Williamson writes:

"According to ancient Asian philosophy, life is not a circle but a spiral. Every life lesson that has ever been presented to you (which means everything you have ever been through) will come back again, in some form, until you learn it. . . .

Whatever didn't work in your life before this point was a re-flection of the fact that you hadn't yet integrated the different parts of yourself. . . . Broken parts of you encountered broken parts of others. . . . That was then and this is now."

Holy heck.

If I'd been paying attention, this is nothing new. I could have, and should have, learned this in my Christian upbring-ing or just through life in general. So many of us, though, wipe our brow after getting through a rough patch basically caused by our own lack of intellect and then move on without thinking about the lesson learned.

Naturally, some people are better at this than others. I'm sure there are many of you who are thinking, "Well, I've made a mistake or two in my life, but I learned from it and I never did it again." Good for you! Some of us are just a little bit pokier.

I bring this up not to insult those of us who have taken our sweet time to mature, but to show that at some point—through our own perseverance and not just through luck—the maturity kicks in. And for many of us, the maturity arrives in waves. You may grow up quickly in some ways but remain childlike in others.

The important part, as Williamson notes in her book, is to learn from your mistakes so you can move on. How many times do I repeat the same mistake over and over? For instance, my husband has a calendar on which he writes every single purchase we make. And he has been telling me for, I don't know, fifteen years to write down all of my purchases. This helps him to budget and to see where we might be spending too much money. But I'm lazy, and I don't do it right away. Without fail, at the end of the month, I'm scrambling to re-member what I've spent the past thirty days so I can write it down before the credit card bills arrive. Also without fail, I forget something, and it's usually a big purchase. And then my husband asks, with an appropriate amount of impatience, why I don't write down expenses as soon as they are made.

What can I say? I continue to be lazy. If I take Williamson's words to heart, one day this is going to have some bigger consequences for me unless I finally get my act together and write down all of my expenses. This is part of my maturing process, one that most people would have assumed I'd adopted a lot sooner. So, okay, Marianne, that was yesterday. Today, I start writing everything down!

What I enjoy most about getting older is that I always seem to be a little better than I was before. I guess that is a result of my slow maturing process. I finally feel comfortable in my own skin. I'm not as shy as I used to be. I don't blow situations out of proportion like I used to (although my family might debate that). I'm not so self-absorbed.

There's still more work to be done, of course. At this rate, I will enter full maturity sometime in my seventies. I hope I have at least another decade or so after that to enjoy it.

CHAPTER 15
DON'T LOOK BACK IN ANGER

The 1991 movie *Defending Your Life* tells the story of two people who die and must reflect on their lives to determine if they will enter the pearly gates or return to earth to start all over. The man, played by a hilarious actor named Albert Brooks, has his work cut out for him. Not that he was a bad person; he was just more of a putz, always doing things halfway and never quite learning from his mistakes. In fact, he meets his demise while trying to remove a disk from his car's CD changer and gets into a fatal accident.

Spoiler alert: Brooks' character is a half-second away from getting kicked back down to earth, but then he rescues an altruistic character played by Meryl Streep, and they both get to enjoy eternity together. The point is that, sometimes even up until the end we're still trying to get it right. And maybe just the idea that we're *trying* means we're not doing that bad of a job.

If this guide could ensure that you'd never make a regretful move in your life, it would be worth its weight in gold. Truthfully, no matter how many "do this/don't do that" books or articles you read, an instance will no doubt arise where you make a move you wish you hadn't. My hope is that those moves are relatively minor in the grand scheme of things, and that your memories will be more about good actions and experiences.

This advice is for those times when you zig instead of zag. Or you don't zag fast enough or far enough. You may realize this five minutes or five years after it happens. A miscalculation, a careless mistake, a desire to make something happen even if it wasn't meant to be—whatever the reason, you'll mess up a bit, and that's usually okay.

The important thing is to learn from your mistakes; hopefully, the first time they happen. I would love to say that I never erred after an initial mistake. In many instances, that hasn't been the case, which is why I've taken the time to write this book. Sorting through what worked and what didn't in my life has helped me to see things much more clearly—that's called hindsight. And my hindsight can become your foresight.

With that in mind, here are some seemingly ordinary yet incredibly helpful things to remember, even though I've had a hard time remembering them myself. Most should be self-explanatory, but that doesn't mean they're easy to do (at least for me):

- Don't leave your keys in a different place every time you come home.
- Don't get back into a relationship with someone who treated you badly before unless you like reliving unpleasant experiences.
- Don't accept every credit card invitation that lands in your mailbox.
- Don't try to make things better for others by taking on everything yourself.
- Don't operate a motorized vehicle on less than four hours of sleep.
- Don't conduct a professional phone call on less than four hours of sleep.
- Don't hold grudges.
- Don't roll your eyes when your parents talk.
- Don't roll your eyes when your kids talk.
- Don't let your driver's license expire.
- Don't feel sorry for yourself.
- Don't write a professional letter of introduction on a sheet of your child's filler paper.
- Don't get mad when someone beats you at something you're good at.
- Don't change your opinion because you're worried about what others will think.
- Don't show up for an important appointment with your only writing implement being a Strawberry Shortcake

pen. If you do, don't brag about the ink actually smelling like strawberries.

· Don't tell yourself there's no time to call a friend, visit a sick relative, make a special dinner for someone.

· Don't ever—ever—pull an all-nighter.

Let's end this on a positive note. For every self-deprecating story in this book, there are at least two success stories. Some of them seem inconsequential to me, but as a whole, they illustrate a life lived better than even I would admit.

So, here are some "dos" in my personal experience that you may want to embrace:

· Do worry about what your parents think. Doing so will likely keep you out of trouble.

· Do volunteer your time. There's no better way to get out of your own head.

· Do take trips, with someone else or on your own. It may be the opportunity of a lifetime.

· Do strive to be better and better—without putting too much pressure on yourself.

· Do go out of your way to help others, even if there is a level of inconvenience for you.

· Do get a dog. Or a cat. Or a guinea pig. Or some other animal that you can hug and talk to when humans just aren't cutting it.

· Do teach, tutor, or coach so that you can share your talents with others and make a difference in someone else's life.

· Do try to make other people smile or laugh.

· Do keep your spirituality or go back to it if you've fallen away.

· Do treat your family members like they are the most important things in the world, because they are. You can also sometimes treat them like they're annoying, because they can be. But they're the most significant annoying people you will ever know.

- Do make lots of different friends.
- Do cry when the need arises. If the need arises too often, talk to someone.
- Do read books, magazines, blogs, cereal boxes— anything to stimulate your mind.
- Do write in cursive. It can be a defining element of your personality.
- Do show empathy and compassion any time it's appropriate.
- Do listen to music. Again, it's the mind stimulation thing.
- Do eat dessert every now and then.
- Do learn a foreign language. Then take a trip where that language is spoken.
- Do give hugs.

Life has good moments and bad ones. The key to keeping the bad ones at bay is to learn from them and to focus on the good experiences. That is a lesson that I am still trying to master, and hopefully I can get there before time runs out.

But you—you have plenty of time to learn, grow, and be the best you can be. Start early and keep at it. And if you're ever wondering how *not* to handle a situation, I hope you'll flip open this book. I also hope you won't have to do it that often.

THE END

ACKNOWLEDGMENTS

Thank you to my children for holding me accountable to finally get a book written and published after more than fifteen years of saying I would. Thanks to my husband for giving me the opportunity to write while also raising our children.

Special thanks to Lisa Bess Kramer of Cleveland Edits for her expert editing and advice.

Finally, many thanks to all of the people who have put up with me over the years. The list is too long to fit here.

CPSIA information can be obtained
at www.ICGtesting.com
Printed in the USA
LVHW012327100121
675857LV00006B/944